FOREWORD

Dear Reader,

Welcome to *Little Riddlers - Poets From Scotland*, are you ready to get your thinking caps on to puzzle your way through this wonderful collection?

Young Writers' Little Riddlers competition set out to encourage young writers to create their own riddles. Their answers could be whatever or whoever their imaginations desired; from people to places, animals to objects, food to seasons. Riddles are a great way to further the children's use of poetic expression, including onomatopoeia and similes; as well as encourage them to 'think outside the box' by providing clues without giving the answer away immediately.

All of us at Young Writers believe in the importance of inspiring young children to produce creative writing, including poetry, and we feel that seeing their own riddles in print will keep that creative spirit burning brightly and proudly.

We hope you enjoy riddling your way through this book as much as we enjoyed reading all the entries.

Allie Jones

Little RIDDLERS

Poets From Scotland

Edited By Allie Jones

First published in Great Britain in 2018 by:

Young Writers
Remus House
Coltsfoot Drive
Peterborough
PE2 9BF
Telephone: 01733 890066
Website: www.youngwriters.co.uk

Book Design by Ashley Janson

SB ISBN 978-1-78896-018-2
Printed and bound in the UK by BookPrintingUK
Website: www.bookprintinguk.com
YB0342BZ

CONTENTS

Newtongrange Primary School, Newtongrange

Jamie McCann (7) 136
Rebecca Gonzalez (7) 137
Lachlan Robert Goad (7) 138
Isla Cunningham (7) 139
Cameron John Stables (7) 140
Ben Starke (7) 141
Aimee Milliken (7) 142
Julia Wijata (7) 143
Georgia Kaygusuz (7) 144
Sean Jones (7) 145
Kenzie James Fox (7) 146
Niamh Wilson (7) 147
Sasha Muvuti (7) 148
Kayla Bennett (7) 149
Josh Marc Metcalfe (7) 150

St Bridget's Primary RC School, Baillieston

Ryan Woods (6) 151
Cole M (7) 152
Ava Burrows (7) 153
Shaun Burns (6) 154
Rosie Gaughan (7) 155
Cole Grant (7) 156
Sarah Grady (6) 157
Noah Mackay (6) 158
Declyn Brockett (7) 159
Caleb John Gilbride (7) 160
Beth Marley (6) 161
Romia Lawlor (6) 162
Hira Dar (7) 163
Lucas Bradley (6) 164
Lewis Ferrie (6) 165
Sarah Cahill (7) 166
Joseph Jude Howard (6) 167
Ava McCormick (7) 168
Jack Robert Docherty (7) 169
Caoimhe Cocozza (6) 170
Lennon Owens (7) 171
Jessica Reilly (7) 172
Aaron Jacobs (7) 173
Lennon Nicol (7) 174
Lucas Cullen (7) 175
Hana Bilal (7) 176
Ella Paxton (7) 177
Miyah Mowat (6) 178
Ollie Burnett (7) 179
Sara Bumba (7) 180
Mark Docherty (7) 181
Caitlin O'Hanlon (6) 182
Kayden Docherty (7) 183
Ethan James David Williams (7) 184
Tawina Chakana (6) 185
Liam Christopher Barr (7) 186
Chloe McWhirter (7) 187
James Dickson (6) 188
Emma Fraser (6) 189

St Leonards Junior School, St Andrews

Kamilah Muqit (7) 190
Ishbel Jackson Lyons Reid (6) 191
Cara Lang (6) 192
Paula Timmins (6) 193
Ruben Loe (6) 194
Mohamed Attia (7) 195
James Wright (6) 196
Bella Timmins (6) 197
Meredith Munro (6) 198
Marta Anderson (6) 199
Cara Easton (7) 200
Hayfaa Al Ajami (6) 201

Warout Primary School, Glenrothes

Holly Morrison (6) 202
Ethan McElhinney (6) 203
Millie Speed 204
Aleksej Visovens (6) 205
Emma Stewart (6) 206
Austin Mackay (6) 207

Woodside Primary School, Silvertonhill

THE POEMS

Rolling On The Beach

I roll and bounce
And I am lots of fun.
You kick me and it will not hurt.
I'm as bouncy as a frog
And as round as a harvest moon.
These are the sounds I make,
Boing, splat, whack and *shuffle*.
What am I?

Answer: A beach ball.

Mairi Walmsley (7)
Aboyne Primary School, Aboyne

Halloween Time

My eyes are as sharp as a spy.
You see me at Halloween.
I move as slowly as a tortoise.
My teeth are as sharp as spikes.
I will try to scare you by moaning.
I might jump and say, 'Boo!'
What am I?

Answer: A zombie.

Aaila Banks (6)
Aboyne Primary School, Aboyne

Broom, Broom

I have a spoiler at the top.
I have an engine.
I have four wheels.
I go *broom, beep, vroom.*
I use petrol like a motorbike.
I drive people like a bus.
What am I?

Answer: A car.

Ethan Cruickshank (6)
Aboyne Primary School, Aboyne

Eyes In The Sky

I have wings.
My body is covered in feathers.
My eyes are as sharp as a spy.
My sounds are *squawk* and *rrrrrr*.
I can fly as high as a kite.
What am I?

Answer: *A bird.*

Emilia Keith (6)

Aboyne Primary School, Aboyne

Bouncy Riddle

I have webbed feet.
I am bumpy.
I am bouncy.
I like leaping.
I boing like a bouncy ball.
I am springy like a kangaroo.
I have little teeth.
What am I?

Answer: A frog.

Harry Dempster (6)
Aboyne Primary School, Aboyne

The Hopping Thing

I hop and I boing.
I ribbit, ribbit, ribbit.
I hop from lily pad to lily pad in a slimy pond.
I boing as high as a kite,
Then splash in the water.
What am I?

Answer: A frog.

Daisy Gardyne (5)
Aboyne Primary School, Aboyne

Baa, Baa

I am black, white and fluffy.
I live in the field.
I have four legs.
I eat grass.
I go 'baa, baa'.
I am small like a goat.
What am I?

Answer: A sheep.

Emma Martin (6)
Aboyne Primary School, Aboyne

A Crackle In The Sky

I am bright.
I am light.
I make a very loud noise.
I bang and crackle.
I am smoky and colourful.
I crackle in the sky.
What am I?

Answer: *A firework.*

Hannah Garden (6)
Aboyne Primary School, Aboyne

Flying High

I am as big as a plane.
I am green.
I roar very loudly.
I breathe fire.
I fly through the sky as fast as a seagull.
What am I?

Answer: A dragon.

Zac Bates (5)
Aboyne Primary School, Aboyne

Fluffy Pet

I have fluffy ears
And I bounce like a beach ball.
I have a cute face.
I eat carrots.
I squeak and I wiggle my nose.
What am I?

Answer: A bunny.

Olivia Vegh-Reti (5)
Aboyne Primary School, Aboyne

Fantastic Fruit

I am yellow.
I am squishy.
I am yummy.
You peel me.
You can slip on my skin.
I'm as bendy as a boomerang.
What am I?

Answer: A banana.

Fraser Blair (6)
Aboyne Primary School, Aboyne

Special Visitor

I have wings.
I visit at night boys or girls.
I leave gifts.
I flutter.
I'm as sparkly as glitter.
Who am I?

Answer: The tooth fairy.

Erin Thomson (6)
Aboyne Primary School, Aboyne

Wagging Tail

I dig and bark.
I am as big as a desk.
I am playful.
I can be as hairy as a highland cow.
I can wag my tail.
What am I?

Answer: A dog.

Lewis Leil (5)
Aboyne Primary School, Aboyne

Sweet Treat

I am soft and cold.
I am different colours and flavours.
I am frozen like ice.
You can lick me and suck me.
What am I?

Answer: Ice cream.

Rhys Thomson (5)
Aboyne Primary School, Aboyne

The Flying Candy

I am as pink as candyfloss.
I make a tinkle when I fly.
I eat glitter.
I fly.
I have a sparkly tail.
What am I?

Answer: A unicorn.

Darcey Yule (6)
Aboyne Primary School, Aboyne

Super Swimmer

I eat fish.
I play spy jump.
I live with a pod in the sea.
I click.
I am as grey as rain.
What am I?

Answer: A dolphin.

Louise Catherine Gray (6)
Aboyne Primary School, Aboyne

Hit The Road

I have wheels.
I rev and I vroom.
I'm as fast as lightning
And as comfortable as a sofa.
What am I?

Answer: A car.

Gabriel Kowalski (6)
Aboyne Primary School, Aboyne

Woof!

I woof and find socks.
I run and fetch stones.
I'm as soft as a feather.
I wag my tail.
What am I?

Answer: A dog.

Rylan Fraser Stewart (5)
Aboyne Primary School, Aboyne

The Pet

I bark and dig.
I have fur.
I have paws but no claws.
I am as fluffy as my toy.
What am I?

Answer: A dog.

Harry Ewen (6)
Aboyne Primary School, Aboyne

Help To Eat

I clink.
I'm sharp.
I help you to eat.
I am as silver as metal.
What am I?

Answer: Cutlery.

Jack Gordon Barrie (6)
Aboyne Primary School, Aboyne

Beat So Fast

I beat so fast
And I dream as a strawberry.
I go *boom, boom.*
What am I?

Answer: A heart.

Dominik Erdodi (6)
Aboyne Primary School, Aboyne

Half Full

I am as cold as ice.
You drink from me.
I am hard but I can smash.
What am I?

Answer: A bottle.

Cian Thomas Beverley (6)
Aboyne Primary School, Aboyne

Me Flying

I am yellow and black.
I fly.
I am fuzzy like a pom-pom.
What am I?

Answer: A bee.

Ferghus McPherson (6)
Aboyne Primary School, Aboyne

Water King

He eats possibly everything in his way.
He takes up a whole bank of fish.
He takes up all of your swimming space.
He lives in the sea.
He has tiny eyes.
He could hold a thousand people on his back.
What is he?

Answer: A whale.

Liesbeth Semple (8)
Athelstaneford Primary School, Athelstaneford

As Green As Grass

It is tall.
It's as green as a sea turtle.
It is as beautiful as a puppy.
It is as tall as the sky.
The leaves change colour.
It has branches.
What is it?

Answer: A tree.

Cara Lai (7)

Athelstaneford Primary School, Athelstaneford

The Fast Runner

She is crazy.
She is silly.
She is fast.
She is annoying.
She is jumpy.
She is licky
And she goes *whoosh*.
She poops and pees.
What is she?

Answer: *My puppy.*

Emma Daisy Delahooke (7)
Athelstaneford Primary School, Athelstaneford

Smelly House

It is very quiet.
It is as small as an ant.
It is as smelly as poo.
It is more dangerous than a lion.
It is as brown as mud.
It twitches its nose.
What is it?

Answer: A mouse.

Lewis Fallowfield (8)
Athelstaneford Primary School, Athelstaneford

Sleigh Time

He is like a dad.
He wears black and red.
He likes whisky.
He is as kind as a grandpa.
He goes down the chimney.
He goes, 'Ho! Ho! Ho!'
Who is he?

Answer: Santa.

Maisie Grace Calder (8)
Athelstaneford Primary School, Athelstaneford

The Good Animals

It barks and it chews.
It bites and it is fluffy.
It is bigger than a cat.
It licks and it woofs.
It likes biscuits.
It likes to jump.
What is it?

Answer: A dog.

Ava Loudon Lee (8)
Athelstaneford Primary School, Athelstaneford

Rooftopper

I am as cute as a bunny.
I am very flexible.
I love milk.
I am as daring as an acrobat.
I am as fast as a cheetah.
I am very agile.
What am I?

Answer: A cat.

Amber Duncan (7)
Athelstaneford Primary School, Athelstaneford

A Hopping Friend

It is lovely.
It can jump.
It is cute.
It is as happy as a hare.
It makes a twitchy sound.
It has a fluffy tail.
What is it?

Answer: A bunny.

Suzie Stark (6)

Athelstaneford Primary School, Athelstaneford

Squeaky Friend

He is cute.
He is funny.
He is fluffy.
He eats a lot.
He squeaks.
He likes being lifted up.
What is he?

Answer: A guinea pig.

Isla Fallowfield (6)
Athelstaneford Primary School, Athelstaneford

Family

He is a good swimmer.
He gets me takeaways.
He is as fast as a cat.
He is fun.
He takes me to places.
Who is he?

Answer: My daddy.

Aniyah Khan (7)
Athelstaneford Primary School, Athelstaneford

Fluffy

He has four legs.
He has a wiry coat.
He jumps.
He barks loudly.
He has fluffy ears.
He bites.
What is he?

Answer: A puppy.

Isla Zanre (6)
Athelstaneford Primary School, Athelstaneford

The Slither

It is black.
It is bitey.
It is scaly.
It is sneaky.
It can camouflage.
It is wet.
What is it?

Answer: A snake.

Jack Thomson (7)

Athelstaneford Primary School, Athelstaneford

The Fluffiest

I am so, so cute.
I am fluffy.
I am fun, fun, fun!
I am cuddly.
I am funny.
I bark.
What am I?

Answer: My dog.

Lauren Leslie (7)
Athelstaneford Primary School, Athelstaneford

Strong Winds

I'm made out of wind.
I spin.
I suck things up and break stuff.
Good thing is, I'm a type of weather.
Strong winds sound like a speeding train.
I'm a funnel shape.
I can be found anywhere.
I'm tall like a mountain.
I go round and round very fast.
I look a weird funnel shape.
I am mostly in America.
What am I?

Answer: A tornado.

William Mowat (7)
Broomhill Primary School, Aberdeen

My New Best Friend

Love giver
Care receiver
Command obeyer
For food player
Paw shaker
Rule breaker
Crazy jumper
Order tamper
Bark master
Who runs faster
Ball catcher
Shoe snatcher
Deep digger
Fun trigger
Toy sorter
Loud snorter
Grrr growler
Awoo howler

Tail wagger
Fluffy hugger
Obedience perfector
Home protector
What am I?

Answer: A dog.

Abbie Radaczynska (7)
Broomhill Primary School, Aberdeen

Fly It

I am made out of paper.
I come in different designs.
My owner is good at folding.
You can fly me for miles.
I fly like a bird.
Teachers don't like me if you make me.
I go *whoosh* when I go by.
It is easy to throw me.
What am I?

Answer: A paper plane.

Morgan Christie (7)
Broomhill Primary School, Aberdeen

Round And Round And Round I Go

I swim with the fish.
I fly up high in the sky.
When I move I am too small to see.
When it's cold I'm as hard as a stone.
I just keep on going round and round.
I make noises like *drip, splash* and *splosh*.
What am I?

Answer: A water drop.

Ella Tatler (7)

Broomhill Primary School, Aberdeen

Not Two-Tyred

I can go fast.
I have a single wheel.
I'm used in circus performances.
I have a metal frame.
I am the world's tallest at 114 feet.
I can be as tall as a giraffe.
I can go *whoosh*.
I have pedals but no chain.
What am I?

Answer: *A unicycle.*

Finlay MacDonald (7)
Broomhill Primary School, Aberdeen

Anubis Rules!

Organs missing.
Ancient as the stars.
As old as the hills.
Bandages all over.
Amulets of magic.
Makes jumps and frights.
Canopic jars.
Life after death.
As scary as each other.
Silently sleeping.
What am I?

Answer: An ancient mummy.

Kirsten Turner (7)
Broomhill Primary School, Aberdeen

A Sparkle Surprise

I am hard to find.
I am different colours
But I mostly come in white.
I have four legs and I live in the forest.
I have something spiky on my head.
I run as fast as the wind.
My name is as sparkly as sequins.
What am I?

Answer: A unicorn.

Evie Williams (6)

Broomhill Primary School, Aberdeen

Mr President

I've got brown furry skin
And a soft velvet snout,
Four padded paws
To picnic about.
I've got small beady eyes
That watch over you at night,
As I flick out the light
And hug you tight.
What am I?

Answer: A teddy bear.

Eden Alexander (7)
Broomhill Primary School, Aberdeen

Hop

I am furry.
I have big ears.
You can cuddle me.
I have a little cute tail.
I have thumpy feet.
I have a little cute nose.
I have whiskers.
I have little eyes.
What am I?

Answer: A rabbit.

Iona Beth McHardy (7)
Broomhill Primary School, Aberdeen

I Change A Lot

I can be happy.
I can be sad.
I can be noisy.
I can be angry.
Some people like me.
Some people don't.
All I can say is
I change a lot.
What am I?

Answer: The weather.

Timothy Borisov (7)
Broomhill Primary School, Aberdeen

Animal

I am sometimes yellow.
Sometimes I can be brown.
You can find me in ponds.
I love to eat bread.
I like to fly and swim.
Quack, quack, quack!
What am I?

Answer: A duck.

Jed Logan (7)
Broomhill Primary School, Aberdeen

I Wish For This

I have a tail.
You can take me for a walk.
You can play with me.
I like to play in the garden.
I need a lead to keep me safe.
I can bark loudly.
What am I?

Answer: A dog.

Sienna Smith (7)
Broomhill Primary School, Aberdeen

Wise

I live in trees.
I can turn my head round and round.
I am fluffy.
I am normally brown.
I rustle in the trees.
I can fly like an aeroplane.
What am I?

Answer: An owl.

Sophia Bruce (7)
Broomhill Primary School, Aberdeen

The Speed Machine

I have wheels.
I am fast.
I come in many different colours.
I am powered by the feet.
I can do many stunts.
I am cool.
I can brake.
What am I?

Answer: A bike.

Harris Wilson (7)
Broomhill Primary School, Aberdeen

The Fairy-Tale House

A princess lives there.
There's richness and much more
And a bugle goes *ta, ta, ra, ra, ra*.
It's beautiful.
It's big.
What is it?

Answer: A castle.

Laura Santos Franchin (7)
Broomhill Primary School, Aberdeen

Wheeling Round, Round

You can ride on me.
You can go on adventures with me.
Really good riders do stunts with me.
I am fast and fun.
I have two little wheels.
What am I?

Answer: A scooter.

Harry Davidson (7)
Broomhill Primary School, Aberdeen

Fast And Fun

I have two wheels.
I have handlebars.
I have a seat.
I have lights.
I am like a small car.
My rider needs a helmet.
What am I?

Answer: A motorbike.

Tristan Gunawan McCathie (7)
Broomhill Primary School, Aberdeen

Fluffy Fun

I am fluffy.
I am cute.
I am sporty.
I am fun.
I like to run.
I like to fetch.
I come in some different colours.
What am I?

Answer: A dog.

Timmy Bates (7)
Broomhill Primary School, Aberdeen

At Grannie's House

With colourful feathers
And a medium beak
In his cage he likes to sit!
He likes tea biscuits
At Grannie's house.
With Grandad he talks
Like, 'Are you okay?'
And then he flies and has a play!
What is he?

Answer: A parrot.

Oliver Smith (6)
Fishermoss Primary School, Portlethen

Little Perry

He might live in a safari park.
You don't usually find him out in the dark.
He roars out loud
When food is found.
With his great big paw
He holds it on the ground!
What is he?

Answer: A bear.

Maya Robertson (6)
Fishermoss Primary School, Portlethen

Hopscotch

In the park, in the sun,
He loves to have fun!
He is good at hopping
And eats carrots.
He plays with his friends.
When he gets tired
He sits and eats his carrots.
What is he?

Answer: A rabbit.

Lucy Beth Firmin (6)
Fishermoss Primary School, Portlethen

Ocean Blue

I kind of like tricks.
I love lots and lots of fish.
I like to swim free
And dive through the air
Back into the sea!
I swim with my friends in a pod like peas!
What am I?

Answer: A dolphin.

Grace Whitfield (6)

Fishermoss Primary School, Portlethen

Brownie

He is brown
With great big eyes!
He has great big ears
And is very wise!
Brown and feathery,
What does he do?
Apart from a loud tu-whit tu-whoo?
What is he?

Answer: An owl.

Klaudia Hagyariova (5)
Fishermoss Primary School, Portlethen

Rainbow Dash

With colourful wings
It can fly.
It looks so pretty
Crossing the sky.
Colours of the rainbow,
What a show!
In the sky it seems to glow.
What is it?

Answer: A butterfly.

Hanna Bogunia (5)
Fishermoss Primary School, Portlethen

Feathered Friend

It talks.
It copies me.
It copies sounds going around the house.
It sounds like the phone
But no one is there.
Just me and some feathers!
What is it?

Answer: A parrot.

Madison Handsley (5)

Fishermoss Primary School, Portlethen

Maxi

In the water he will go
To get cooler and have fun!
He paddles with his four legs...
And then he shakes...
Then splashes about when he comes out!
What is he?

Answer: A dog.

Josh Milnes (6)
Fishermoss Primary School, Portlethen

Fluffy

I live in the jungle.
I like to hunt.
I'm a type of cat
With a loud grrrrr!
I'm as tall as a lion
But I can pounce...
100 miles!
What am I?

Answer: A tiger.

Aiden Taylor (6)
Fishermoss Primary School, Portlethen

Stripy

This cat was hungry,
He ate some meat.
This cat was tired,
He went to sleep.
He has stripes,
Orange and black.
He grumbles a lot!
What is he?

Answer: A tiger.

Aaron Brown (5)
Fishermoss Primary School, Portlethen

The Pest

He is a menace!
He likes to fight!
He also likes to pull my hair.
He likes to be a big boy!
I like it when he plays with me!
My pal!
Who is he?

Answer: My brother.

Gemma Stephen (6)
Fishermoss Primary School, Portlethen

Floppy

It has pointed ears.
It has a white, fluffy tail
And shining eyes
That look around
Trying to find...
Carrots...
On the ground.
What is it?

Answer: A rabbit.

Jack Thompson (5)
Fishermoss Primary School, Portlethen

Sammie

He has no legs.
He does have a handle.
He has no arms.
He does have a spout.
He does not talk...
He lets the hot drink pour out!
What is he?

Answer: A teapot.

Jamie Milne (5)
Fishermoss Primary School, Portlethen

Lazybones

It has a furry collar
And a big loud roar.
Roooar!
It likes to eat meat
And lie in the sun!
It has baby cubs who run!
What is it?

Answer: A lion.

Lilly Robertson (6)
Fishermoss Primary School, Portlethen

Sammy

He moves on one foot
And looks quite cute,
As he creeps along
With his house on his back.
He is strong
And he is really tiny.
What is he?

Answer: A snail.

Daniel Tadjiev (6)
Fishermoss Primary School, Portlethen

Ted

He has a long tail!
When he smells the cheese
Which he loves
He twitches,
His whiskers flash
And he runs over
In a dash!
What is he?

Answer: A rat.

Anne Williams (6)
Fishermoss Primary School, Portlethen

Open Sea

I live in the sea.
I am bluey-grey.
I'm clever!
I can be trained to jump through hoops
But I like to swim free in the sea.
What am I?

Answer: A dolphin.

Aiden Robertson (6)
Fishermoss Primary School, Portlethen

The Tree Poem

He lives in a tree!
He sits and twits
As he looks down at me!
He sees a mouse
And he makes a pounce!
Yum, yum, yum!
What is he?

Answer: An owl.

Aston Dobinson (6)
Fishermoss Primary School, Portlethen

Uni Twinkle

I have a single horn
And magical powers!
I've got two wings
But look a bit like a horse
Which I'm not of course.
What am I?

Answer: A unicorn.

Maisie Annabel Stewart (6)
Fishermoss Primary School, Portlethen

Jumbo

A transport that does not go on land.
It has no fingers and no hands
It has big wings
And flies with the birds that sing!
What is it?

Answer: An aeroplane.

Amar Dogra (5)

Fishermoss Primary School, Portlethen

Cheeky Chap

All brown
With a tail.
He loves to eat bananas!
He likes to play
In the trees all day
And he loves to eat bananas!
What is he?

Answer: A monkey.

Jackson Pirie (5)
Fishermoss Primary School, Portlethen

By The Sea

He has a green face
With two eyes and a mouth.
On his back is his house, his shell,
To live in the sea!
In the sea.
What is he?

Answer: A turtle.

Russ Thomson (5)
Fishermoss Primary School, Portlethen

Napper

Often muddy and green.
He is hard to be seen.
With his long snout
And jaws open wide
He wants food inside.
What is he?

Answer: A crocodile.

Lucas Webster (5)

Fishermoss Primary School, Portlethen

Magic

High in the sky
I love to fly!
My lucky horn
Sits on my head
And sometimes annoys me
In my bed!
What am I?

Answer: A unicorn.

Gracie Thornton (6)

Fishermoss Primary School, Portlethen

Max

He likes to swing
In the tree.
He says *oo oo aa!*
Very loudly!
Who is he?

Answer: A monkey.

Finlay Dundas (6)
Fishermoss Primary School, Portlethen

Cheeky Boy

I am as naughty as a crocodile.
I am horrible to Perfect Peter.
I can turn into a dinosaur.
I am horrible to my friends at school.
I am always up to mischief.
I have messy brown hair.
Who am I?

Answer: Horrid Henry.

Violet Eve Patrick (6)
Greenhill Primary School, Coatbridge

Cheeky Snapper

I am sneaky like a robber.
Snap, snap, snap, snap, snap.
My teeth are razor-sharp.
Lots of teeth are in my mouth.
I swim around in the water.
I lie down waiting.
What am I?

Answer: A crocodile.

Lily Burns (6)
Greenhill Primary School, Coatbridge

Razor Teeth

I am as big as a house.
I have big sharp teeth.
I can swim like a fish.
Under the water is where I live.
I go *snap, snap, snap.*
My fin is on my back.
What am I?

Answer: A shark.

Mason Gibson-Murphy (6)
Greenhill Primary School, Coatbridge

Gallop

I can jump.
I can run like the wind.
I live in a stable.
I go *clippety-clop*.
I have long hair on my head and tail.
I come in lots of colours.
What am I?

Answer: A horse.

Eva Mortimer (6)
Greenhill Primary School, Coatbridge

Big Cat

I might try to eat you.
I might try to scratch you.
I run as fast as a cheetah.
I have sharp teeth.
I have sharp claws.
I have black stripes on me.
What am I?

Answer: A tiger.

James Morgan (6)
Greenhill Primary School, Coatbridge

Secret Cave

From my ghost you will be free.
A map takes you to me.
My lock is skulls.
I am filled with gold coins.
I creak open.
I am made with wood.
What am I?

Answer: A treasure chest.

Lewis Fraser (5)
Greenhill Primary School, Coatbridge

A Wavy Thing

I wave in the wind.
I feel like a brick rock.
I come in different sizes.
I am covered in leaves.
I can be bigger than houses.
I swish in the wind.
What am I?

Answer: A tree.

Aden Hunter (6)

Greenhill Primary School, Coatbridge

Cute

I boing about all the time.
I am fluffy like a dog.
I am cute like a cat.
I am an animal with long ears.
I like to eat carrots.
I live outside.
What am I?

Answer: A rabbit.

Leah Fleming (6)
Greenhill Primary School, Coatbridge

Fast

I have black wavy hair.
I have a long hairy tail.
I live in the field.
I can jump over a fence.
I am as fast as a cheetah.
Neigh!
What am I?

Answer: A horse.

Kamryn Carlyle (6)
Greenhill Primary School, Coatbridge

Fluffy

I have a fluffy tail.
My ears are as big as leaves.
I like to hop around.
I am fluffy like the clouds.
Bop!
I have pointy ears.
What am I?

Answer: A rabbit.

Mila Quinn (6)
Greenhill Primary School, Coatbridge

The Fluffy Tail

My tail is fluffy as a cloud.
I like carrots.
I have sharp claws.
I go *boing, boing, boing.*
I live on the grass.
I am so soft.
What am I?

Answer: A rabbit.

Giorgia Negro (6)
Greenhill Primary School, Coatbridge

Fluffy

I drink milk.
My fur is fluffy like a rug.
I can be lots of different colours.
I have sharp claws.
I can purr really loud.
I love to jump up.
What am I?

Answer: A cat.

Nathan Maxwell (6)
Greenhill Primary School, Coatbridge

Silky

I have sharp teeth.
My coat is silky and shiny.
I have four legs.
I love to walk and play.
My bark can be loud.
My tail wags when I am happy.
What am I?

Answer: A dog.

Tyler Beattie (6)
Greenhill Primary School, Coatbridge

Rolling

I have four legs.
I am very smooth.
I have a round nose.
I live in a pen.
I have a tummy like a beach ball.
Oink, oink, oink.
What am I?

Answer: A pig.

Sophia Dowridge (6)
Greenhill Primary School, Coatbridge

Rosy

I am happy because I am red.
I grow in trees.
I am rosy.
I can be red or green.
I can have seeds.
I am round like a beach ball.
What am I?

Answer: An apple.

Millie Gardner (6)

Greenhill Primary School, Coatbridge

Big Wings

I am as scary as a bear.
My wings are very big.
I live in a castle.
My eyes are very scary.
I am red.
My throat is very hot.
What am I?

Answer: A dragon.

Logan Adair (6)
Greenhill Primary School, Coatbridge

The Woods

I can eat other animals.
I make a weird screaming noise.
I have black eyes.
I can look like a wolf.
I can be found in the woods.
I am as orange as a carrot.
What am I?

Answer: A fox.

Lucy Leonard (7)
Greenhill Primary School, Coatbridge

Black And White

I am fluffy like a teddy.
My claws are sharp.
I am very cute.
I like milk.
Miaow, miaow, miaow.
I chase mice.
What am I?

Answer: A cat.

Jacob Cochrane (6)
Greenhill Primary School, Coatbridge

Fast Ride

I go fast.
I am fun.
I go up and down.
I like to move.
People are scared of me.
I am really, really good.
What am I?

Answer: A roller coaster.

Ava Welsh (6)
Greenhill Primary School, Coatbridge

Scratchy

I have whiskers.
I am fat.
I have fur.
I scratch you when you lift me.
I have a long tail.
I sleep like a baby.
What am I?

Answer: A cat.

Mia Welsh (6)
Greenhill Primary School, Coatbridge

Fat Pet

It loves milk.
It is black.
It is fluffy.
It has a long tail.
It has sharp claws.
It is a house animal.
What is it?

Answer: A cat.

Olivia Welsh
Greenhill Primary School, Coatbridge

The Crazy Monster

I am brown like a bear.
I live in a tree.
I am as crazy as a kid.
I love bananas.
Some people think I am cute.
I jump about like a kid.
What am I?

Answer: A monkey.

Elliot James Bell (7)
Greenhill Primary School, Coatbridge

Sleepy

I like to sleep.
My eyes' colour is green.
I eat meat.
I can live outside or inside.
I like milk.
My tail is as long as a lion's.
What am I?

Answer: A cat.

Victoria McCloy (7)
Greenhill Primary School, Coatbridge

The Jaggy Flower

I am jaggy.
I need the sun.
I live outside.
I have petals.
I need water.
I come in different colours.
What am I?

Answer: A rose.

Madison Tierney (6)
Greenhill Primary School, Coatbridge

Soft Things

I live in a house.
I am a pet.
I live in a hut sometimes.
I like to play with balls.
I have four paws.
I have little claws too.
What am I?

Answer: A dog.

Kai Best (6)

Greenhill Primary School, Coatbridge

A House

My house is small.
I am small but you can still see me
I can be a pet.
I like to eat cheese.
I have a tail.
I have four legs.
What am I?

Answer: A mouse.

Sam Finnigan (6)
Greenhill Primary School, Coatbridge

The Farm

I have four legs.
I am as fluffy as a cloud.
I have two eyes.
I eat grass.
I drink water.
The sound I make is *baa*.
What am I?

Answer: A sheep.

Christopher Noble (6)
Greenhill Primary School, Coatbridge

Fluffy Things

I am as fluffy as a pillow.
I live in a house.
I eat treats.
I make a growling sound.
I run very fast.
I play with sticks.
What am I?

Answer: A dog.

Olivia Gwynneth Henderson (7)
Greenhill Primary School, Coatbridge

The Crocodile

I have four legs.
I have sharp teeth.
I have two green eyes.
I live in water.
I eat fish.
I make a snap, snap noise.
What am I?

Answer: A crocodile.

Daniel Loudon (6)
Greenhill Primary School, Coatbridge

Magic Animal

I have wings.
I am pink.
I am beautiful and cute.
I can fly.
I am magic.
I have a mane.
What am I?

Answer: A unicorn.

Darcii Young (6)
Greenhill Primary School, Coatbridge

Wild Animals

I have four legs.
I am as fast as a cheetah.
Some people think I am cute.
I like grass.
I like humans.
I have blue eyes.
What am I?

Answer: A dog.

Kai Jeffrey (7)
Greenhill Primary School, Coatbridge

The Zoo

I am as tall as a house.
I eat leaves.
I can live in a zoo.
I stamp like an elephant.
I am smooth like a snake.
I am yellow and orange.
What am I?

Answer: A giraffe.

Elsie Mae Newstead (7)
Greenhill Primary School, Coatbridge

Bouncer

I am fluffy.
I make a boing.
I jump.
I am white.
I eat carrots.
I have pointy ears.
What am I?

Answer: A rabbit.

Cody Roberts (6)
Greenhill Primary School, Coatbridge

Spotty

I live in a house.
I eat fish.
I am as fluffy as a sheep.
I can be black and white.
I have four legs
I have a tail
What am I?

Answer: A cat.

Kaelen McGuire (6)
Greenhill Primary School, Coatbridge

Soft

I am fluffy.
I have big ears.
I jump up and down.
I have floppy ears.
I make a boing noise.
I have little paws.
What am I?

Answer: A rabbit.

Declan William Jones (6)
Greenhill Primary School, Coatbridge

The Underwater Wild

I am the colour blue.
I eat meat.
I am strong.
I have black eyes.
I am wild as a whale.
I live underwater.
What am I?

Answer: A shark.

Keelin McPherson (7)
Greenhill Primary School, Coatbridge

The Pink Kill

Winter flies.
Walks on water.
Bug eater.
Three toes.
Hot feathers.
Fluffy.
What am I?

Answer: A duck.

Daniel Hamill (6)
Greenhill Primary School, Coatbridge

The Wild

I like bananas.
I like people.
I like to play.
I live in the jungle.
I go crazy.
I live in the trees too.
What am I?

Answer : A monkey.

Sophie Young (6)
Greenhill Primary School, Coatbridge

Nice And Soft

I am black.
I have green eyes.
I am fluffy as a sheep.
I have ears.
I am small.
I am soft.
What am I?

Answer: A cat.

Ava Thom (6)

Greenhill Primary School, Coatbridge

The Sea King's Daughter

I swim in the sea
And I have lots of fishy friends.
I live in a castle and I sing like a whale.
I have a rainbow tail with flowers.
My dad is the king and my mum is the queen.
I can pretend that I am a superhero.
I love to paint pictures
But the paint comes off the paper.
Who am I?

Answer: A mermaid princess.

Cayla Alexis Samson (6)
Lady Alice Primary School, Port Glasgow

The Football Master

I am the bestest footballer.
I am a right-winger.
I play for Barcelona and I also play for
Argentina.
I have red, purple and white football boots.
My Argentina strip is blue and white.
I am a real person.
When I score I shout, 'Yes! What a goal!'
Who am I?

Answer: Lionel Messi!

Callum Mitchell Greenan (6)
Lady Alice Primary School, Port Glasgow

The Black Hat

I have a black hat.
You can't see me.
I have a sword.
I sail on the seven seas.
I demand orders to my crews.
I have a wooden leg.
I have a grey, bushy beard.
I wear an eye patch.
I am very lazy.
I kill people.
I steal treasure.
Who am I?

Answer: A ghost pirate.

Ruairidh McLellan (6)
Lady Alice Primary School, Port Glasgow

Gru's One-Eyed Servant

I am yellow like the sun.
I like bananas like a monkey.
My T-shirt is blue like a Smurf.
Some of us have one eye.
I am silly like a clown.
I serve Gru.
I have 1,000,000 brothers.
My master has three daughters.
My master is a criminal.
Who am I?

Answer: A Minion.

Dylan McGinness (6)
Lady Alice Primary School, Port Glasgow

The Crafty People

It's blocky.
You can do a tutorial.
There are two modes.
There are mods.
There are updates.
You can hunt and build.
My noise is like *nee-noo, nee-noo, nee-noo.*
I'm as tall as a box.
What is it?

Answer: Minecraft.

Kyle Melvin (6)
Lady Alice Primary School, Port Glasgow

Under The Water

I am the best animal in the water.
I swim very deep so no one can catch me.
I eat fish and seaweed.
I can talk like people.
I can swim like a dolphin.
I love to hide in small places.
What am I?

Answer: A mermaid.

Layla Mealey (7)
Lady Alice Primary School, Port Glasgow

Flying Wings

My fur is grey and fluffy,
It is beautiful.
I have a big black nose.
I have a good scent.
I am beautiful.
I have a big rainbow horn.
I have lots of magic.
What am I?

Answer: A unicorn.

Honor Mollie Watson (7)
Lady Alice Primary School, Port Glasgow

The Rolling Rocket

It is juicy.
It lives in someone's stomach.
It has a stick on the top.
You do hear it when you peel the skin off.
I have a brown bit when you take my skin off.
What is it?

Answer: An orange.

Filip Jacher (7)
Lady Alice Primary School, Port Glasgow

Pegasus

I fly high in the sky.
I eat clouds.
I shoot out rainbows when I fly.
I hate water.
I like the sun.
I live in a castle.
What am I?

Answer: A unicorn.

Nivanna Rice (6)
Lady Alice Primary School, Port Glasgow

Colourful Journey

I have two wheels.
I have a seat.
I have bristles.
I like all colours.
I move slowly.
I use paper.
What am I?

Answer: A bike paintbrush.

Liam McCreath (8)
Lady Alice Primary School, Port Glasgow

What Am I?

I go *woof, woof* all day.
I go out for walks.
I drink water.
I eat dry food.
I'm happy all day.
I am funny.
I'm cute, cuddly and snuggly.
What am I?

Answer: A dog.

Tailahleigh Bow (7)
Miller Primary School, Glasgow

What Am I?

I am as red as fire.
I have green hair.
I have lots of seeds.
I am tasty.
You will think I am the best
And also I am red and ready to go.
What am I?

Answer: A strawberry.

April Deans (7)
Miller Primary School, Glasgow

The Cold Day

It is cold but fun.
We can build snowmen.
It is white all around.
We like it.
We like throwing it at each other.
We can ice skate on the ice.
What is it?

Answer: Snow.

Emilia Mrzyglod (6)
Miller Primary School, Glasgow

The Greatest Football Player Ever

He kicks a football.
He's fast
But sometimes he's slow.
He's good at shouting 'who are you?'
Who is he?

Answer: Ronaldo.

Kai Alexander Clark (7)
Miller Primary School, Glasgow

Food Is Amazing

I am sweet and red.
Also healthy.
I am a fruit.
I am amazing.
I have seeds.
What am I?

Answer: A strawberry.

Nate Nicolson (6)
Miller Primary School, Glasgow

What Am I?

I am tasty and very yummy.
I am a fruit that is yellow.
You can peel me.
What am I?

Answer: A banana.

Anna Leaman (6)
Miller Primary School, Glasgow

Elemental Kid

He is strong.
He is a powerful element.
He can fly
And he can shoot fireballs out of his hands.
He has spiky hair.
He's got cool outfits.
He turns into Super Saiyan.
He has got a strong body.
Who is he?

Answer: Goku Junior.

Jamie McCann (7)
Newtongrange Primary School, Newtongrange

Teenage Witches

They do magic.
They fight against each other with magic.
They don't have wands.
They have soft voices.
They tinkle when they cast a spell.
They are pretty like snow in winter.
What are they?

Answer: *Teenage witches.*

Rebecca Gonzalez (7)
Newtongrange Primary School, Newtongrange

The Green Creature

It is green like grass.
It is small like a bird.
It is camouflaged like glass.
It can climb trees like a monkey.
It is scary like a bat.
It lives in the forest like a wild animal.
What animal is it?

Answer: A dinosaur.

Lachlan Robert Goad (7)
Newtongrange Primary School, Newtongrange

Animals In The Wild

It is hot like Spain.
It has trees like a rainforest.
A lot of animals live there.
The grass is green like leaves.
It makes a swoosh sound.
It sometimes makes a crash, bang, thump noise!
What is it?

Answer: A jungle.

Isla Cunningham (7)
Newtongrange Primary School, Newtongrange

The Funny Person

It looks funny.
It is cool like a monkey.
It is hot like an African desert.
It juggles fire.
It rides on a one-wheeled bike.
It is good at balancing.
It is good at making balloons.
Who is it?

Answer: A clown.

Cameron John Stables (7)
Newtongrange Primary School, Newtongrange

The Explosion

He is an evil man.
He has magical powers.
He has a good wife.
His brother is a fighter with magical powers.
He has special powers.
He could blow up a skyscraper.
Who is he?

Answer: Vegeta from Dragon Ball.

Ben Starke (7)
Newtongrange Primary School, Newtongrange

Green Like Grass

It's crunchy like popcorn.
It's like a little green tree.
It crunches like carrots.
It's like a pea.
It's soft like a bunny.
It's crunchy like crisps.
What is it?

Answer: Broccoli.

Aimee Milliken (7)
Newtongrange Primary School, Newtongrange

Fishing Time

It flies low, diving in the water.
It flies like a bird.
It sounds swishy.
It glides like the wind.
It flies like a woodpecker.
It swims as quickly as a shark.
Who is it?

Answer: A flying fish.

Julia Wijata (7)
Newtongrange Primary School, Newtongrange

The Strange Animal

It is colourful.
It is as huge as a giraffe.
It is an unusual strange animal.
It starts with a P.
It is colourful like a rainbow.
It has bright feathers.
Who is it?

Answer: A peacock.

Georgia Kaygusuz (7)
Newtongrange Primary School, Newtongrange

The Yellow Fellow

He is as yellow as a dummy.
He is as yellow as the golden sun.
He is as funny as a clown.
He loves to dance.
He loves ice cream.
He runs very fast.
Who is he?

Answer: SpongeBob.

Sean Jones (7)
Newtongrange Primary School, Newtongrange

A Fluffy Ball

I purr growingly.
I eat tasty fish and mice.
I am furry like a sheep.
I have sharp whiskers.
My tail helps me balance.
I am a meat eater.
What am I?

Answer: A cat!

Kenzie James Fox (7)
Newtongrange Primary School, Newtongrange

Frozen

She is as cold as a snowflake.
She is like snow.
She is like a marshmallow.
She is a girl.
She has a sister.
She is young like a child.
Who is she?

Answer: Elsa.

Niamh Wilson (7)
Newtongrange Primary School, Newtongrange

Magic Time

I am magic.
I am a queen.
I have ice powers.
I'm beautiful and I have blonde hair.
I have a sister.
I wear a blue dress.
Who am I?

Answer: Elsa.

Sasha Muvuti (7)
Newtongrange Primary School, Newtongrange

Cheesy Vegetable

I am like a tree.
I like cheese on top.
I am crunchy.
I am small.
I am yellow.
I look like broccoli.
What am I?

Answer: A cauliflower.

Kayla Bennett (7)
Newtongrange Primary School, Newtongrange

The Green Monster

He is green.
He is sticky.
He is bad.
He is in a movie.
He is messy.
He has white teeth.
Who is he?

Answer: Slimer.

Josh Marc Metcalfe (7)
Newtongrange Primary School, Newtongrange

Superstar Rumble

'You can't see me,' is his catchphrase.
He fights for glory which is why he can amaze.
He is a wrestler and it makes him a champ.
He hardly ever does a stamp.
He is a champ as well as a superstar.
He fights to go to Wrestlemania
But to go he must go far.
Who is he?

Answer: John Cena.

Ryan Woods (6)
St Bridget's Primary RC School, Baillieston

Scary Creature

I am big but sometimes small.
I make webs too.
I crawl around dark places.
You see me running around with eight legs.
You can't survive my teeth!
It takes a long time for me to make my webs
So don't break them!
What am I?

Answer: A spider.

Cole M (7)
St Bridget's Primary RC School, Baillieston

The Rainbow Animal

On its head is a horn
And for breakfast it has corn.
Some people don't believe they're real
But I think their magic I feel.
It eats all different kinds of sweets.
The noise it makes is bleats.
What is it?

Answer: A unicorn.

Ava Burrows (7)
St Bridget's Primary RC School, Baillieston

Super Stadium

You play with a ball,
Sometimes you might fall.

You play on a pitch,
Sometimes you might get a stitch.

Sometimes the ball might go in the goal,
Sometimes the ball might get stole.
What is it?

Answer: Football!

Shaun Burns (6)
St Bridget's Primary RC School, Baillieston

Bathroom Essential

You can use it if you're wet
And you can also use it on your pet.
It is best when it's dry,
But you can also use it on a warm pie.
You can use it, it is soft.
You can also use it as a cloth.
What is it?

Answer: A towel.

Rosie Gaughan (7)
St Bridget's Primary RC School, Baillieston

Bite, Bite, Bite

I live in the sea.
I am as scary as jumping off a skyscraper.
I have sharp teeth and they are big.
I am as fast as a dolphin.
I make a scary noise, it is loud.
I am enormous, bigger than a dolphin.
What am I?

Answer: A shark.

Cole Grant (7)

St Bridget's Primary RC School, Baillieston

Scary, Scary

I'm as scary as a plane crash.
I'm as funny as a comedian.
I'm as happy as a kid eating sweets.
I'm sometimes as sad as someone falling.
You sometimes dress up.
I'm a celebration.
What am I?

Answer: Halloween.

Sarah Grady (6)
St Bridget's Primary RC School, Baillieston

I Am A Good Cook

I am industrious and amazing.
I am outstanding and clever.
My hair is as black as the night sky.
My dress is green as a sea turtle.
My husband works in the lighthouse.
I make delicious food.
Who am I?

Answer: Mrs Grinling.

Noah Mackay (6)
St Bridget's Primary RC School, Baillieston

Freaky Fruit

When you peel my skin
It goes in the bin.
When I am ready my skin is yellow.
When you eat me I will be a happy fellow.
It is the minions' favourite thing to eat.
The minions dance to the beat.
What is it?

Answer: A banana.

Declyn Brockett (7)
St Bridget's Primary RC School, Baillieston

Safe Seaside

The thing has to be tall
And it helps the boats to not fall.
At the top there is a light.
If you want to clean it you must have might.
It is very helpful
And the keeper sits on a stool.
What is it?

Answer: A lighthouse.

Caleb John Gilbride (7)
St Bridget's Primary RC School, Baillieston

Pedal, Pedal

I can be as fast as a cheetah.
I can be coloured any colour.
I have a soft seat.
I have pedals that go round and round.
You can add a horn on the front of me.
I have brakes on the front of me.
What am I?

Answer: A bike.

Beth Marley (6)
St Bridget's Primary RC School, Baillieston

Colourful Creature

I am a beautiful insect.
I live in lovely leaves.
I go for a long sleep.
When I wake up I turn colourful.
Before I wake up I turn colourful.
I can fly like a bee.
What am I?

Answer: A caterpillar then a butterfly.

Romia Lawlor (6)
St Bridget's Primary RC School, Baillieston

Halloween Queen

My character is scary.
She is the opposite of a fairy.
Her house is very spooky
And be careful children, she might cook you.
She goes on a broom
And she can't ride it in her room.
Who is she?

Answer: A witch.

Hira Dar (7)
St Bridget's Primary RC School, Baillieston

Fantastic Football

He is a good striker.
He is as fast as a biker.
He can beat the keeper.
Crowd cheers out of the speakers.
He can score a goal with a ball.
Because he is tall, he can climb up walls.
Who is he?

Answer: Messi.

Lucas Bradley (6)
St Bridget's Primary RC School, Baillieston

Super Season

The weather is very sunny
And the bees give you honey.
The weather is very hot
And lots of sun cream will be bought.
I go to Lanzarote on holiday
Where you can eat gummies.
What is it?

Answer: Summer.

Lewis Ferrie (6)
St Bridget's Primary RC School, Baillieston

Singing Star

You will hear a sound.
If I scream I would be found.
The choir uses it to sing.
If you lost it, it would be a terrible thing.
It is loud.
It makes my mum and dad very proud.
What is it?

Answer: A voice.

Sarah Cahill (7)
St Bridget's Primary RC School, Baillieston

Wobble, Wobble

When I dive I splash.
I swim really fast.
I love to eat fish.
I can dive really fast.
I'm black and white.
I have an orange beak.
I keep my baby under me.
What am I?

Answer: A penguin.

Joseph Jude Howard (6)
St Bridget's Primary RC School, Baillieston

Perfect Present

I am as colourful as a rainbow.
I need sun and rain.
I smell as good as perfume.
I am beautiful.
I am sometimes on the ground.
Sometimes you keep me in your house.
What am I?

Answer: A flower.

Ava McCormick (7)
St Bridget's Primary RC School, Baillieston

The Animal Game

The animals hide
But you can catch it outside.
A Pokéball helps
But be careful, the sand will melt.
They hunt for food
And the Pokéball is good.
What is it?

Answer: A Pokémon.

Jack Robert Docherty (7)
St Bridget's Primary RC School, Baillieston

Super Season

The snow is cold.
Wear a hat and scarf you're told.
The water turns to ice.
Ice skating would be nice.
It could sometimes be wet.
It might be too cold for your pet.
What is it?

Answer: Winter.

Caoimhe Cocozza (6)
St Bridget's Primary RC School, Baillieston

Tiny Bite

I am here, but you can't see me.
I start with the letter A.
I am as strong as a strong man.
If I crawl on you I will bite.
I tickle a bit.
I am a food thief.
What am I?

Answer: An ant.

Lennon Owens (7)

St Bridget's Primary RC School, Baillieston

Big, Bad Sea Monster

I can shoot litres of water.
I eat seals.
My teeth are as sharp as a crocodile's.
I live in very deep water.
I am as black as leather.
I am not scary.
What am I?

Answer: A killer whale.

Jessica Reilly (7)
St Bridget's Primary RC School, Baillieston

Soggy Day

I make an annoying sound.
I might drop water on you.
I make a mess outside.
Sometimes I'm dark
And sometimes I'm light.
Sometimes I blow umbrellas away.
What am I?

Answer: A cloud.

Aaron Jacobs (7)
St Bridget's Primary RC School, Baillieston

Fun Food

They are very tasty.
I eat them very hastily.
I eat them with chips.
I lick my lips.
You can get them from McD's.
You can get them with cheese.
What are they?

Answer: Chicken nuggets.

Lennon Nicol (7)
St Bridget's Primary RC School, Baillieston

YouTube Vlogs

He has a dog.
To watch him you must log.
In his house he acts very silly.
He stays in his house when it is very chilly.
He waves.
He is very brave.
Who is he?

Answer: Jake Paul.

Lucas Cullen (7)
St Bridget's Primary RC School, Baillieston

Helpful Cupboard

After you eat you wash your dishes.
If you want you can get wishes.
It can be tall.
It can clean you when you fall.
It can make you dry.
Goodbye.
What is it?

Answer: A towel.

Hana Bilal (7)
St Bridget's Primary RC School, Baillieston

Floating Friend

I am as slow as a snail.
I am as white as snow.
I float as high as a skyscraper.
Sometimes I'm grey or white.
I am as fast as a teddy bear.
What am I?

Answer: A cloud.

Ella Paxton (7)
St Bridget's Primary RC School, Baillieston

The Sea Princess

She wants to be on land.
She wants to stand.
Her prince is called Eric.
The movie is perfect.
Her talent is to sing.
She swims but has no fin.
Who is she?

Answer: Ariel.

Miyah Mowat (6)
St Bridget's Primary RC School, Baillieston

Fake Fun

He is on TV
And fights in WWE.
He defeated Sheamus
And is very, very famous.
His tag partner is his brother
And they have the same mother.
Who is he?

Answer: Jeff Hardy.

Ollie Burnett (7)
St Bridget's Primary RC School, Baillieston

Furry Friend

I am as lazy as a turtle.
I live in a house.
I am as small as a pigeon.
I love to sleep all day.
I am as fat as a football.
I drink milk.
What am I?

Answer: A cat.

Sara Bumba (7)
St Bridget's Primary RC School, Baillieston

I Bite

I am as silver as a watch.
My teeth are sharp!
I live underwater.
My fin is sharp!
I have black eyes.
I am as scary as a nightmare.
What am I?

Answer: A shark.

Mark Docherty (7)
St Bridget's Primary RC School, Baillieston

Beaming Building

I am as red as a tomato.
I am as white as a sheet.
I am stripy.
I glow in the night.
I am very tall.
I guide ships past rocks.
What am I?

Answer: A lighthouse.

Caitlin O'Hanlon (6)
St Bridget's Primary RC School, Baillieston

One Slice

I am as round as a wheel.
My edge is brown and crusty.
I am Italian.
I look yummy.
I am red and yellow.
I am as hot as chilli.
What am I?

Answer: A pizza.

Kayden Docherty (7)
St Bridget's Primary RC School, Baillieston

Sticky

I am as black as coal.
I suck your blood.
I live in a swamp.
I am dirty.
I stick to people's skin.
I live in dirt.
What am I?

Answer: A leech.

Ethan James David Williams (7)
St Bridget's Primary RC School, Baillieston

Little Pet

I am as little as a cat.
I squeak every day.
I like walking.
I have sharp nails.
I don't like cats.
I eat cheese.
What am I?

Answer: A mouse.

Tawina Chakana (6)
St Bridget's Primary RC School, Baillieston

Funny L

He is cool.
He has a pool.
He is big.
He sees a girl, her name is Mig.
He is silly.
His name is not Billy.
Who is he?

Answer: Logan Paul.

Liam Christopher Barr (7)
St Bridget's Primary RC School, Baillieston

Adventurous Creatures

I am as yellow as the sun.
As small as a shoe.
I'm as crazy as a monkey.
Hardworking too!
I am funny.
Who am I?

Answer: A Minion.

Chloe McWhirter (7)
St Bridget's Primary RC School, Baillieston

Night Knight

My man is a knight.
He gets a sword to fight.
Castles he will raid.
He is dangerous.
Who is he?

Answer: Black Douglas.

James Dickson (6)
St Bridget's Primary RC School, Baillieston

Hickity Hockity

I am big.
I eat carrots.
I eat hay.
I chew like a camel.
I am an animal.
What am I?

Answer: A horse.

Emma Fraser (6)
St Bridget's Primary RC School, Baillieston

The Old Duster

You put it on the floor or the carpet.
You can also use it for a tower
Or for patting clothes.
You use it to make things clean.
They used it in olden days to dust the carpet all night.
Then the next day they had to start all over again.
What is it?

Answer: A carpet beater.

Kamilah Muqit (7)
St Leonards Junior School, St Andrews

The Statue

I have a head.
I am as tall as a person.
I sing a song like this: *tick-tock.*
I am as brown as a conker.
I spin all day.
I have a key; you have to turn it.
I have a door on my tummy.
I am as hard as wood.
What am I?

Answer: A grandfather clock.

Ishbel Jackson Lyons Reid (6)
St Leonards Junior School, St Andrews

The Metal Stone

I am made out of metal and stone.
I make your clothes hot.
I am as heavy as a rock.
I have a handle.
You can put me on your clothes.
I have a triangle on the bottom of me.
You have to be strong to lift me.
What am I?

Answer: An iron.

Cara Lang (6)
St Leonards Junior School, St Andrews

An Old Cleaner

You heat it in the fire.
You use it for clothes.
Be careful with it, it is hot!
It is as quiet as a mouse.
It is black and has a handle.
You can use it for flattening your clothes.
What is it?

Answer: An iron.

Paula Timmins (6)
St Leonards Junior School, St Andrews

It's Music!

I am as small as a little packet of tissues.
You can blow me.
I am shiny.
I have lots of lines inside me.
There are words written on me.
When you blow into me I shout.
What am I?

Answer: A harmonica.

Ruben Loe (6)
St Leonards Junior School, St Andrews

The Metal Man

I am shiny.
I have got a spiky sword.
I have got armour.
I am sparkly.
I have a helmet.
My armour and helmet are grey.
My armour is as hard as a rock.
Who am I?

Answer: A prince.

Mohamed Attia (7)
St Leonards Junior School, St Andrews

The Big Fire-Breather

It is a big thing.
It is a scary thing.
It can breathe fire and be mean.
It is naughty and as scary as a giant.
It has a scaly tail.
What is it?

Answer: A dragon.

James Wright (6)
St Leonards Junior School, St Andrews

The Great Machine

I can do stitches.
I go up and down.
There was a grandmother working me.
You use me to make stitches in your clothes.
What am I?

Answer: A sewing machine.

Bella Timmins (6)
St Leonards Junior School, St Andrews

The Crunchy Hard Thing

I am kind of shiny brown
And a hard metal.
You can roll me.
I have a handle.
I am used to clean.
I am very hairy.
What am I?

Answer: A mop.

Meredith Munro (6)
St Leonards Junior School, St Andrews

The Shiny Musical Thing

I sing.
I am shiny metal.
I am musical.
I am hard.
I am a little bit colourful.
You hit me with beaters.
What am I?

Answer: A xylophone.

Marta Anderson (6)
St Leonards Junior School, St Andrews

The Happy Swimmer

I am as brown as a conker.
I have spots and I live in the water.
I am as green as a branch.
What am I?

Answer: A stingray.

Cara Easton (7)
St Leonards Junior School, St Andrews

The Web Weaver

I like to spin and eat leaves.
I like to eat flies.
I make webs.
What am I?

Answer: A spider.

Hayfaa Al Ajami (6)
St Leonards Junior School, St Andrews

Stalker

Eighteen sharp claws that tear
Lava orange fur with black
A loud scary roar
Brown eyes that find you at night
Stalking, pouncing and attacking.
What is it?

Answer: A tiger.

Holly Morrison (6)
Warout Primary School, Glenrothes

Vroom

Black tyres
Shiny and big
Stopping, forwards, backwards
A human needs to control me
It's a machine.
What is it?

Answer: A car.

Ethan McElhinney (6)
Warout Primary School, Glenrothes

Stripes

London
Black and white fur
Eating, running, looking
Love the stripes going down the sides.
Grasslands.
What am I?

Answer: A zebra.

Millie Speed
Warout Primary School, Glenrothes

Fun

My toy
Metal rainbow
Spinning, slowing and stopping
Smile, calm and annoying noise
Plaything
What is it?

Answer: A fidget spinner.

Aleksej Visovens (6)
Warout Primary School, Glenrothes

Small

Small, light, colourful
My wings are symmetrical
Flying, landing, eats pollen.

What is it?

Answer: A butterfly.

Emma Stewart (6)
Warout Primary School, Glenrothes

Playing

Build and pull apart
Hard, bumpy, colourful bricks
A horse or a robot.
What is it?

Answer: Lego.

Austin Mackay (6)
Warout Primary School, Glenrothes

What Is It?

It has zips on it.
It has different colours on it.
It keeps my water bottle in it.
It has my homework in it.
I put it on my back.
Some are big and some are small.
What is it?

Answer: A bag.

Hannah Frances McBrearty (6)
Woodside Primary School, Silvertonhill

Who Am I?

I wear a black suit
And a black mask.
At night-time I jump out.
When I'm ready to battle
I use my toys.
I like bats.
I don't like bad guys.
Who am I?

Answer: Batman.

Zac Mirrlees (6)
Woodside Primary School, Silvertonhill

Who Am I?

I have two black beady eyes.
I have big hairy claws.
I like to catch and scare mice.
I am always out at night.
I have a prickly back.
Who am I?

Answer: The Gruffalo.

Amy Campbell (6)
Woodside Primary School, Silvertonhill

What Am I?

I have black wings.
I come out at night.
I fly about people's houses
And I like black skies.
What am I?

Answer: A bat.

Ellie Bokor (6)

Woodside Primary School, Silvertonhill

Who Am I?

I can swing.
I stay in the home.
I can run.
I can beat bad guys.
I spray webs.
Who am I?

Answer: Spider-Man.

David Samuel Pate (5)
Woodside Primary School, Silvertonhill

What Am I?

I cover birds.
You can pet me.
I am fluffy.
Between the fluff I have a stick.
What am I?

Answer: A feather.

Alfie Mckay (6)
Woodside Primary School, Silvertonhill

Deep Sea

I have eight legs.
I have green eyes.
I am purple.
I live underwater.
What am I?

Answer: An octopus.

Layla Fulton (6)
Woodside Primary School, Silvertonhill

YOUNG WRITERS INFORMATION

We hope you have enjoyed reading this book – and that you will continue to in the coming years.

If you're a young writer who enjoys reading and creative writing, or the parent of an enthusiastic poet or story writer, do visit our website **www.youngwriters.co.uk**. Here you will find free competitions, workshops and games, as well as recommended reads, a poetry glossary and our blog.

If you would like to order further copies of this book, or any of our other titles, then please give us a call or visit **www.youngwriters.co.uk**.

Young Writers
Remus House
Coltsfoot Drive
Peterborough
PE2 9BF
(01733) 890066
info@youngwriters.co.uk